GOLDEN
PRIZE

GOLDEN PRIZE

AND OTHER STORIES ABOUT HORSES

COVER ILLUSTRATION BY
DENNIS HOCKERMAN

ILLUSTRATED BY
CLIFF SCHULE

GOLDEN PRESS
Western Publishing Company, Inc.
Racine, Wisconsin

Library of Congress Catalog Card Number: 65-21126

0-307-21508-3

CONTENTS

Golden Prize

Erva Loomis Merow

Terry stood looking at the brightly decorated box in the department store. The big sign beside the box read WIN A SURPRISE PRIZE! JUST SIGN YOUR NAME AND DROP IT IN THE BOX!

"Well, well," said Mr. Cook, the manager of the store. "Did you put your name in the box, little boy?"

"No," said Terry. "May I?"

"Certainly, certainly," said Mr. Cook. "But hurry. I draw a name out in just a minute. You might be the lucky one!"

Quickly Terry wrote his name on the small piece

of paper. *Terry Douglas Smith* he wrote, then dropped the slip into the box. Then he stood and watched.

All at once everyone ran toward Mr. Cook.

"It is time! It is time!" called Mr. Cook, ringing a very loud bell.

My name will be on top, thought Terry. *Maybe. . . .*

But Mr. Cook picked up the beautiful box and shook it and shook it and shook it!

Oh, oh, thought Terry. *My name must be on the very bottom of the box now!*

Mr. Cook opened the box and reached far down inside it.

Terry stood very still.

"The winner," shouted Mr. Cook, ringing his bell, "is . . . Terry Douglas Smith!"

"That's me! That's me!" shouted Terry. "My name is Terry Douglas Smith!"

"Well, well." Mr. Cook laughed. "You are a lucky boy! Look behind you and you'll see your prize!"

As Terry turned to look behind him, a man led

in a beautiful, huge golden horse and tied him in a pen.

"A horse!" shouted Terry. "A real horse!"

"Yes, it is," said Mr. Cook. "Just go up to the office and leave your name and address and tell the girl where you'd like to have your prize delivered. He will be all yours."

Everyone shouted and clapped for Terry. Then they turned back to Mr. Cook, who was about to draw another name for another prize.

Terry just stood there and looked at his golden horse.

"Why," said Terry, "I don't have to have you delivered! I live just around the corner. Come on, horse. Let's go home."

He took the reins and led the horse right out the door and into the street.

"Gee," whispered Terry, "I always wanted a pet. But, a horse! Gee!"

They walked right down the sidewalk.

"Maybe we'd better hurry just a little," said Terry. "I don't know if a horse can walk on the sidewalk or not."

Terry turned at the very next corner and led the horse through the front door of a very large apartment building.

"Come this way," he said. "We'll use the freight elevator."

Up, up, up, and up they went, way to the top of the building.

Terry stroked the horse on his ears and on his nose and under his chin.

"Oh," said Terry, "you are so nice."

The elevator bumped to a stop and the door opened.

"You are much bigger than even a big dog," Terry said to his horse as he led him out of the elevator.

"We're home! We're home," he called, opening the door to his apartment.

To the horse he said, "Come right in, horse!" and led him into the living room.

"Make yourself comfortable," said Terry, "and I'll get something for us to eat. I don't know how you sit down, but I don't think you'd better because there doesn't seem to be much room left now. You just stand right there and I'll hurry back."

He hurried into the kitchen and came back with two large red apples.

"Wheeeeeeeeeeeeeeeeee," said the horse, showing his huge white teeth. In one gulp both apples were gone.

"Gee," said Terry, "you do have big teeth. And one of those apples was for *me!* Oh, well! Are you still hungry? I'll get some cereal."

Before Terry could pour the cereal into a bowl, horse had picked up the box with his teeth. He shook the cereal all over the floor.

And before Terry could pick it up, in walked Mother!

Mother screamed!

Father ran into the living room!

Father shouted, "A horse in our house!"

"I won him," said Terry, as proud as could be.

"You won him?" shouted Father. "You won a *horse?*"

"All by myself," said Terry. "And I have a wonderful name for him."

"You won a *horse?*" said Father, still shouting.

"Yes, sir," said Terry. "Isn't he beautiful?"

"He's—he's very big," said Mother.

"Do you want to hear what I'm going to call him, Mother?" asked Terry.

"Yes, dear," said Mother, still trembling just a little.

"I'm going to call him Golden Prize!" said Terry.

"That—is—a—beautiful name for him," said Mother.

"Did anyone see you come up here?" asked Father.

"No," said Terry. "We used the freight elevator and just walked right on in."

"You can't have a horse in an apartment," said Father. "There must be a law!"

"Do you think so?" asked Terry.

"Oh, I'm sure of it," said Mother. "They are so very big."

"But he's mine," cried Terry. "I *won* him. I *won* him."

"But he's a horse," said Father, "and a very *big* horse, too."

"I don't think I ever saw a bigger one," said Mother weakly.

"But he's my horse and I love him and I'll walk him two or three times a day, just like a dog," cried Terry.

"Where?" asked Father. "On the roof?"

"Oh, no," cried Terry. "He might jump right off! In the alley, by the garbage cans!"

"What would the garbage collectors say when they saw that great, huge animal in the alley?" asked Father.

"I'd be riding him," said Terry, "and they'd say, 'What a lucky boy he is to have a horse of his own!' "

"Oh, no," said Father. "They'd call the police! That's what they'd do."

"Oh-h-h-h-h-h-h," cried Terry, "no, horse, no! *Don't!*"

It was too late. Horse was finishing the last of a beautiful bouquet of flowers. Just the stems stuck out of his mouth.

"I think he's still hungry," said Terry.

"Well, Terry," said Father, "why don't you

phone the grocer and tell him we have a guest? Tell him to send up three steaks, some salad greens, and some ice cream."

"Good," said Terry.

"And," shouted Father, *a bale of hay and sixty bunches of carrots!"*

"He wouldn't believe me," said Terry.

There was a knock at the door.

"Oh," said Mother, "the ladies from the club," and she opened the door quickly.

Too quickly!

The ladies took just one look at the big golden horse standing right there before them, munching on the stems of flowers. They ran screaming down the hall!

"Oh, dear," sighed Mother. "And they were coming for tea."

She looked at Golden Prize.

"How will I ever explain a horse in my living room?" asked Mother. "My lovely tea! Ruined!"

There was a very loud knock at the door.

"The police," said Father and calmly opened the door.

There stood Mr. Kemp, the landlord!

"A horse in my apartment house? *Kerchoooo,*" sneezed Mr. Kemp.

"Why, Mr. Kemp," said Terry, "I thought you were only allergic to cats!"

"Cats—*kerchooo*—and—*kerchooo*—all furry —*kerchooo*—animals—*kerchooo*—and—*kerchooo* —especially—*kerchooo*—horses!" sneezed Mr. Kemp. "OUT—*kerchooo!* OUT—*kerchooo!* OUT —ker—ker—ker—chooooooooooooo!"

He banged the door as he left.

"We'll get him out of here at once," called Father.

"Oh, no," cried Terry. "He's mine. He's mine."

"Maybe the riding stables would like to have him," suggested Mother. "You could go there and ride him anytime you wanted to."

"But he wouldn't be all mine," cried Terry, hanging on to Golden Prize.

"Maybe they still have horses pulling some of the milk wagons in the city," said Father.

"Oh, no," cried Terry. "He'd get so tired! He's mine. He's mine."

"Perhaps they'd let us give him to the zoo," said Mother.

"Oh, no," cried Terry. "He'd be with lions and tigers and he wouldn't know he was mine!"

"Maybe the circus needs a golden horse, Terry," said Father. "Wouldn't you like him to be a circus horse?"

"I'd go with him," cried Terry. "I'd run away with him and be in the circus, too. He's mine! I won him. He's all mine."

The telephone rang and Mother hurried to answer it.

"Hello," said Mother. She listened for a moment. Then she began to laugh.

"She wouldn't laugh if it was a policeman," said Terry.

The longer Mother listened the more she laughed!

Finally she said, "It's Grandfather. He called to tell us he just bought the Merryhill Farm and wants to know if Terry would like to come and spend the summer there."

"Oh-h-h-h-h!" screeched Terry. "Ask him if I

may bring a special friend with me."

"Terry," shouted Mother, "you can't ride a horse in the living room. Now, get down!"

She turned back to the phone. "Yes—yes, Grandfather. A horse! Terry won a horse! I know it's hard to believe, Grandfather, but he *did* it. He won this great big golden horse. Oh —could he? Oh, he'd be so happy, Grandfather! Yes, we'll hire a trailer and be there as soon as possible. Thank you ever so much, Grandfather. Good-bye."

"Oh, did you hear that?" said Terry as Father lifted him off the horse's back. "You're mine! We're going to live on Merryhill Farm and we'll gallop over the hills and through the woods. We'll play cowboys and Indians, and soldiers and knights. And everyone in the countryside will see us and they'll say, 'There goes that brave boy and his *Golden Prize!*' "

Molly Takes a Holiday

Mabel Watts

Molly the mare was not very young. She was not really very pretty. But Mr. Freddy, the fishman, thought her the most willing, the most wonderful, mare in the city.

Every day Molly plodded along, pulling the fish wagon through the streets, while Mr. Freddy called,

> "Fish, fish! Fresh from the sea, from the
> lake, from the river. Fresh as can be!
> Fish, fish, fish!"

People hurried out of their houses when Mr.

Freddy came by with his load of fish.

Cats came out, too. Pet cats and stray cats came out. Fat ones, lean ones, and in-between ones, all came to see Molly and Mr. Freddy.

Mr. Freddy threw pieces of catfish to the cats. And, best of all, he did not charge them a penny!

Winter, summer, spring, and fall the fishman and his mare were always together, no matter what the weather.

One day Mr. Freddy made up a little song about their friendship:

> "We'll stick together, through thick and
> thin. Together, together, we're bound to
> win!"

Molly had many horse friends, too. Horses who pulled ice wagons, junk wagons, and coal wagons were her friends. Horses who pulled bread wagons, milk wagons, and laundry wagons, all knew Molly.

To Molly every day was a grand adventure. She was fond of Mr. Freddy. And she liked the people who bought his fish. She even liked the cats who got their fish and did not pay a penny for it. She was as happy as a horse could be. That is, she was happy until Mr. Freddy decided to take a vacation.

"My throat is getting tired from calling, 'Fish, fish, fish!' " he said. "Tomorrow I'm going to take a train to the seashore!"

Molly could hardly believe her ears. She and Mr. Freddy had been together for years and years. She was too upset to eat her oats.

I deserve a holiday, too, she thought. She tried to tell Mr. Freddy. She nipped his sleeve. She nuzzled his back.

Mr. Freddy laughed. "What's the matter, Molly?" he asked. "Do you want to go, too? A horse on vacation? Never heard of such a thing!"

The seashore would put sparkle in my eyes, thought Molly. *It would bring back my appetite.* She looked at Mr. Freddy with her big brown eyes. Then she laid her head against his arm.

"All right! You win!" said Mr. Freddy.

The next morning he harnessed Molly to the fish wagon and off they went, both in the greatest of spirits.

The old mare clopped happily along, her head held high in the summer sunshine. Today the reins felt loose. Without its load of fish, the wagon felt as light as a feather. There was just Mr. Freddy, his suitcase, and his song:

"We'll stick together, through thick and thin. Together, together, we're bound to win!"

At the seashore Mr. Freddy rented a cozy cottage with a cozy stable for Molly. Gone was the smoky city smell. Instead, there was the salty smell of the sea.

Gone were the busy city sights. Instead, Molly saw the blue and white sky and the blue and white sea. Sea gulls screamed. Tugboats tooted. The waves broke on the shore with a shushing sound.

Molly tingled with excitement. *No harness on my back!* she thought. *No fish wagon to pull! Can this really and truly be me?*

"Let yourself go!" coaxed Mr. Freddy. "Go on, Molly; enjoy yourself! You are on a holiday now."

In the field behind the cottage Molly nibbled at the tender green grass. Here she could kick up her heels and act as silly as she pleased. She could scratch her sides on fence posts. She could roll

on her back. She even swished her tail at some butterflies. Oh, it was a wonderful feeling, being on vacation.

When Mr. Freddy went in swimming, Molly ran along the water's edge to keep an eye on him. Mr. Freddy was not a very good swimmer. He could dog-paddle, after a fashion. But not nearly as well as a dog. And not nearly as far.

One day Mr. Freddy paddled out too far. He reached for the bottom. It was not there. "Help! Help!" he screamed.

A lifeguard heard his call. He splashed through the breakers and swam rapidly toward Mr. Freddy.

Molly followed. She swam for all she was worth. And though she had never taken a swimming lesson in her life, she soon left the lifeguard far behind.

Molly could see her master bobbing up and down. Sometimes she could see him. Sometimes she could not! Faster and faster she swam!

Molly reached Mr. Freddy at last. She grasped his swimsuit between her teeth and pulled him slowly but surely toward shore.

We'll stick together, through thick and thin,

26

thought Molly as she pulled Mr. Freddy through the water. *Together, together, we're bound to win!*

Mr. Freddy grabbed hold of Molly's mane. He tried to sing his song, but he couldn't. *"Glub, glub,"* he gurgled.

At last they were safe and sound on the shore. Once the water had been squeezed out of him, Mr. Freddy felt as good as new.

"You saved my life," he told Molly. "And to think I almost left you at home!"

A crowd began to gather around the brave, courageous mare. A lady fed her sandwiches from a picnic basket. A young girl put a daisy chain around Molly's neck.

The next morning Molly's picture appeared in all the city papers. The mayor saw it as he ate his breakfast.

"A mare on vacation!" he said. "That's something new and different!"

"It's something good!" replied his wife as she ate her cereal. "Horses work hard for their oats, all year long. They need a change and a rest, just as people do."

27

"You are absolutely right," the mayor agreed. "And from now on all horses must be given a yearly vacation! I'll make it official. I'll make it a proclamation."

The mayor kept his word. And from that day forward, special holidays just for horses became a must.

Horses who pulled ice wagons, junk wagons, and coal wagons went on vacations. Horses who pulled bread wagons, milk wagons, and laundry wagons all took a holiday.

"All work and no play is not right," their owners agreed. "For people, or for animals."

"Hurray for Molly!" whinnied all the tired, worn-out city horses.

When her holiday was over, Molly was glad to go back to work again. Everywhere she went people pointed her out. They smiled.

"There goes the mare who saved her master's life," they said. "It just shows what you can do when you have to do it!"

However, in spite of her fame, Molly remained the same kind, gentle animal. Every day she plodded

along, pulling the fish wagon, while Mr. Freddy
called,

>"Fish, fish! Fresh from the sea, from the
>lake, from the river. Fresh as can be!
>Fish, fish, fish!"

Molly the mare was not very young. And she
was not really very pretty. But to Mr. Freddy, the
fishman, she was the most loyal, and, yes, the most
surprising, mare in the city.

Runaway Rob

Peg Bottomley

Every time the carnival moved into a new town, the parade was the same.

First the band marched by. There were only two men in the band. One played bagpipes and the other beat a bass drum. But they made a lot of noise, so the children always came running to see what was happening.

Then came three clowns. They walked on their hands. They did cartwheels. They threw lollipops to the laughing children.

Next the big trucks rolled past on their soft rubber

wheels. They carried a lion, three brown monkeys, one baby monkey, and two zebras.

The following trucks carried all the rides. There were carrousels, a Ferris wheel, a loop-the-loop, bump 'em cars, little red fire engines that had their own bells, and small boats that sailed in a steel pond.

Last in line were the ponies and their carts. Mr. Neill marched proudly beside Jenny. She pulled a cart with red wheels. Her mane and tail were braided with ribbons.

After Jenny came Rosalie, then Tim. Last came the smallest, the youngest, and the most unhappy pony anybody has ever seen. His name was Rob.

Rob was smallest because he was youngest. And he was unhappy because he was always last. By the time his part of the parade passed along a street, there was nobody left to see how proudly he could march. There was nobody for him to say hello to with a nod of his head and a flick of his tail. Most of the children had run ahead to keep up with the piper and drummer, to wave to the clowns, and to feel safely scared of the animals in their cages.

Rob liked to run, too. And he wanted to march with the band and see everything that happened. But he had to walk last, no matter how much fun it was to run!

Rob could not even hear the music because he was so far back. Sometimes, when the wind was right, he could hear the deep *thump, thump* of the drum. But of the bagpipes, there was never a real sound, only a whisper like something once heard in a lovely dream.

This day was especially bad. It was a very small town that the carnival had come to. Only a few children had even seen Jenny before they ran to march with the band.

Rob saw that one little girl had stayed. She was walking along near him. Her name was Polly, and she liked ponies very much. So Rob pranced for her and nodded his head. Polly said hello and walked right next to Rob all the way. They both felt happy about that.

It was a hot day. Rob was thirsty, even though Mr. Neill had given all the ponies a cool drink of water before the parade had started.

Even then, Rob thought, his bucket of water had not come until Jenny, Rosalie, and Tim had each had theirs.

Rob was very tired of being last. The more he thought about it, and the hotter and thirstier he got, the madder Rob became.

When they reached the carnival grounds, Rob stood quietly. He had been trained to do that. Mr. Neill bustled about, getting the ponies under their sunshade and unhitching them from their carts until the carnival opened for the day.

While Rob waited, the little girl, Polly, walked up to him and scratched his ears. Then her mother and father called. It was time for Polly to go home.

So Rob watched Mr. Neill.

He seemed quiet enough, but every once in a while Rob's tail flicked back and forth and his ears moved in jerky little motions.

Jenny was in the shade while Rob was thinking that he did not want to be last any longer.

When Rosalie was being unhitched, Rob just hated his cart with the black seat and plain old brown wheels.

By the time Tim was being given his fresh drink, Rob had decided to run away.

"Well, here you are at last," said Mr. Neill, patting Rob's neck. "I'm sorry I took so long with the others, but you don't mind, do you?" he said as he unhitched the cart.

Yes, I do! thought Rob. He jumped away from Mr. Neill's kind hands and ran back the way he had come.

"Wait, Rob! Come back!" Mr. Neill shouted as he tried to catch Rob. Other carnival men saw what had happened and tried to stop the runaway pony.

But Rob was first in line at last! And he decided that he would like to stay there, so he just ran faster.

A nice-looking street with tall trees along the edge appeared on Rob's left. He turned off the main road and raced up the pleasant street.

Rob kept going up the street until he saw some trees with apples on them beyond a little ditch. He jumped the ditch and went into the orchard.

When Mr. Neill and the other men reached the orchard, they could not see Rob, because he was behind the trees. The apples were sweet and juicy, just what a thirsty pony needed.

So Rob stayed there eating, while Mr. Neill and the others ran past the orchard and up the street.

Soon the men came back, arguing. "He must have gone that way," said Mr. Neill, pointing down still another street.

"We can't look any longer," said the carnival owner. "We've got to get back to open the show for the day."

The others went back to the carnival, and Mr. Neill wandered down the street calling for Rob. After a while, his voice could no longer be heard.

Rob ate another apple. Then he began to walk around to see what sort of town he was in.

All during the day, strange things happened in the small town of Beltagh.

At the carnival, the pony rides were slow. The man who was hitching the ponies to their carts did not seem to know how to do it very well. Children stood in line to have a ride. As their shadows grew longer in the afternoon sun, so did the line.

Mr. Neill, tired and dirty from walking through town all day, had a sore throat because he had been calling so much for Rob.

A birthday party broke up in tears when it was discovered that somebody had eaten not only the whole cake but also the candles.

Three houses away, twin boys splashing in a small wading pool moved over to let a pony take a long drink of water. Rob had found out that cake makes you thirsty, and candles leave a bad taste in the mouth.

By this time, Mr. Neill was very upset. The carnival had to leave the next day. He and the other ponies had to go with it.

Mr. Neill went to the radio station and told the men there what had happened. He asked them to tell the story on their news program. After that, he went to the police station and told the sergeant about it.

While he was still there, the phone rang. The call was from a man who had gone out to weed his carrot garden and discovered he did not have any carrots left.

"It's those children who keep coming through here," he told the sergeant. "I want you to make them stop!"

The sergeant told the man that it might have been a pony who had eaten all the carrots. The man was so shocked he forgot to say good-bye before he hung up the phone.

As the sergeant put down his phone, it began to ring again. This time it was a woman. She sounded very upset.

"What is a person to do if she can't sit in her own backyard without having a horrid, ugly horse with wild eyes come galloping through it?" she demanded.

Poor Rob! He had been so scared when the lady screamed that he had felt he had better leave very quickly.

While the sergeant was trying to explain what had happened, the radio news program made a special announcement. All the grown-ups in town heard it. Soon all the children heard it, too. There would be a reward for the person who found Rob.

Polly was one of the first youngsters to start

looking for Rob. She did not want the money but was afraid that Rob would be scared at being all alone. She took several sugar lumps in her pocket to give to Rob if she should catch him.

As a matter of fact, Rob was not a bit lonely. He was leading another parade!

It started when a traffic policeman got all mixed up when he saw a horse waiting for the red light to change.

Then a group of children saw Rob. When they ran to catch him, he left the main street, thinking again it was nice not to be last any longer.

After Rob came the policeman—whose whistle did not sound as nice as the bagpipes and drum. Then came the children and a long line of cars.

People stood back to watch the parade. Some cheered for Rob to run faster.

The cars left Rob's parade when he decided to go through a ball field. The policeman had to go back to get traffic moving again. And the children were too hot to run any longer, so they stayed to watch the ball game.

All except Polly. She ran as long as she could.

Then she walked. But she kept following Rob. He turned into an alley. But when Polly got there, much later, Rob was nowhere to be seen.

Finally, when nobody had seen Rob for hours, Mr. Neill went back to the radio station. He told the men there that he would give Rob to the first person who could catch him.

"The reason I will give Rob away," he said, "is that I know anybody who works hard enough to find him must really love ponies.

"I think Rob ran away because he was unhappy staying with me. I have four ponies to take care of. I can't give as much attention to each one as I would like to, because it takes too much time.

"Rob is the nicest pony I have ever had, and I am sorry to lose him. But I do think he will be happier if he has a friend to care for him alone."

Mr. Neill also said that he would give the pony cart to the lucky person who could find Rob.

Then a very sad Mr. Neill, who really liked Rob, left the station to get ready to leave town.

Polly and the other children heard the news when they went home that night to dinner. But while the others, all through town, were sitting down to eat, Polly went right back to look some more.

Her mother had said that she had to eat first. But her father laughed and said, "Let her go. She's always wanted a real pony. Maybe now she'll have one!"

This time, instead of just running around and looking, Polly tried to think where Rob might be. Of course, a farm pony would probably go toward open fields. But Rob was not a farm pony. He was used to a lot of music and gay sounds.

In the whole town there was only one place where music was always being played, Polly knew. That was at the big record shop that played music all through the shopping center.

Polly ran down to the record shop, but Rob was not there. Polly could hardly hear the music because there was so much noise across the street. An old building was being torn down so that a new library could be built there.

The music played from the back of the shop, too. Polly decided to listen there while she tried to think where the pony might be.

As she turned the corner, Polly kicked a small pebble. It spun around, then came to a stop—right against a pony's hoof! Rob had decided to get away from the noise, too.

He started to back away when he saw Polly. But then he smelled the two sugar lumps in her hand. He came to her slowly and took the sugar gently with his soft mouth. Polly put her hand out to hold him by his leather halter. "Oh, Rob," she said, "you're my pony now!"

And he still is. Polly's father painted the pony cart with brave new colors, and Rob is proud to pull it.

But he does not pull it last in line anymore. The town has a big parade every Fourth of July. Rob, who is the only pony in Beltagh with a gay, bright cart, leads the parade with Polly, right after the flag. The band comes next. Rob and Polly hear all the music and see everything.

And each year, on the date that Polly found Rob, the pony has a birthday cake. Rob eats the whole cake, except for the candles—he knows all about those!

Lefty, the Wrong-Way Pony

Florence Laughlin

It was a fine summer day at Valley Ranch Camp. The boys came running and shouting down the hill to choose their horses for the morning ride.

Lefty, the youngest pony in the corral, tossed his head and pawed the ground eagerly. Perhaps this time one of the boys would choose *him*.

"Dibs on Queenie!" cried a tall boy named Larry.

"Pepper belongs to me," called another.

One by one the horses were brought out and saddled. Mr. West, the Ranch Camp foreman, helped each boy in turn.

One by one the boys jumped into the saddles. Soon horses and riders were ready to go.

All except Lefty. He stood by himself behind the gate.

Sadly he watched the other horses gallop off down the trail. He knew they would walk through the sweet-smelling forest. He knew they would nibble green grass and drink from cool, sparkling streams.

And I have to stay all alone in this old corral and eat dry oats, Lefty thought, feeling very sorry for himself.

Lefty was as handsome as the other horses. He had a golden-brown coat as sleek as silk. He was as swift as a deer and as surefooted as a mountain goat.

But there was one thing he could not do. He could not turn to the right!

He could turn to the left. He could go straight ahead. When the trail curved a little, this way and that, he got along fine. But whenever there was a sharp right turn to be made, Lefty always shook his head from side to side and refused to take that right turn.

Instead, he would turn to the left and make a little circle. When he came back almost to where he started from, he was turned in the right direction!

It was very embarrassing to the Ranch Camp boys. Nobody wanted to ride Lefty.

"He's spooked!" the boys said. "He's a crazy horse!"

"A horse that won't obey orders isn't much good on a ranch," said Mr. West. "If Lefty doesn't get over this bad habit, we will have to sell him."

Lefty knew he was in disgrace. But he just could not help it. The bad habit had been a part of him for as long as he could remember. *But I wish just once a boy would choose me for his morning ride,* Lefty thought.

He munched some dry oats and waited for the riders to return.

Lefty had almost given up hope when one day a wonderful thing happened. A new boy came running down the hill after the others. His name was Peter. And by the time Peter reached the corral all the horses had been chosen. All except Lefty!

When the boy climbed on Lefty's back, the other

boys all began to laugh at him.

"Poor Pete," they shouted. "He has to ride old Spooky!"

The new boy was surprised. "What's wrong?" he asked. "Lefty looks like a fine horse to me."

"Wait and see," they all chanted.

Peter reached down and patted Lefty's neck. "Don't you mind, old boy," he said softly. "I trust you."

Lefty didn't mind at all. He was too happy. As they galloped away after the other riders, he lifted his head proudly. His mane flowed in the wind. It was great fun to carry a boy on his back. Peter laughed with joy, and Lefty liked that.

Everything went fine at first. Lefty sniffed the sweet pine-scented air and heard the ground ring beneath his hooves.

Everything went fine until they came to the first sharp right turn on the trail. The little horse suddenly balked.

"What's the matter, Lefty?" Peter asked. "Come on." He pulled on the reins. He pressed Lefty's side with his heel.

But the pony would not obey. Instead, he turned to the left and made his foolish little circle.

The other boys were watching. They pointed and hooted. "Crazy horse! Crazy horse!" they yelled.

Lefty hung his head in shame. The new boy turned red, but he was not angry. He talked gently to the pony.

"I understand now, Lefty," he said. "When you were a foal, something on the right side of the trail must have scared you. But there's nothing to be afraid of now!" They were riding down the trail again. "Nothing at all."

After that, every day when the boys came down to the corral to choose horses, Peter picked Lefty. He had made up his mind to cure the pony of his bad habit.

First he tried to bribe Lefty, with sugar lumps, to turn to the right. It was no use.

Then he tied a long rope to the pony's neck and tried to pull him to the right. Lefty broke away and made his little circle to get back to his friend.

One morning Peter put on a Halloween tiger mask. He jumped at the pony from the left side so that he would run the other way.

Lefty was not fooled. He just circled to the left and came straight to Peter and nuzzled the boy's shoulder.

Peter gave him a sugar lump anyway.

"It's no use, Peter," said Mr. West. "Lefty will never change. Tomorrow we'll sell him and get a horse who can turn both left and right."

That morning, as Peter rode Lefty down the trail, he never laughed once. "This is our last ride, old fellow," he said.

Lefty sensed his sadness and plodded along with his head down.

It was a hot day. The boys decided to swim in the mountain stream. The current was swift, so Mr. West warned them to be careful.

While the boys swam and played, the horses wandered down to the edge of the river. They crowded together, half in and half out of the water. Lefty saw Peter swimming across the river.

He bent his head to drink.

All at once Lefty heard a familiar voice cry, "Help! Help!" It was Peter's voice!

The little horse perked up his ears to listen. He was sure now! *Peter was in trouble!*

Lefty could see Peter downstream, struggling in the current.

Now the boy was clinging to a rock. He was having a hard time hanging on.

"Come, Lefty!" Peter called.

Lefty twisted around, trying to make his little circle. But he could not! The other horses blocked his path. There was only one way to go. *Straight to the right!* And Lefty did it. He had to reach Peter!

With a twist of his wiry golden-brown body, he broke away from the other horses. He splashed toward the wild water where Peter struggled. He got there just in time.

Peter caught the dangling reins and pulled himself into the saddle.

As Lefty brought his young rider back, a happy yell went up from the other boys. "Lefty did it!" someone cried. "He finally turned to the right!"

"If he did it once, he can do it again," Mr. West said quietly. He helped Peter down from the saddle. "And best of all, he saved Peter from that dangerous current. He saved Peter's life."

Peter put his arm around Lefty's neck. The other boys ran up to admire the pony. They were not laughing now.

Lefty was happier than he had ever been in his life. He had conquered his bad habit. He would not turn to the right for a reward of sugar lumps. He could not even be scared into turning to the right. He had done it for love.

Dancer Carries Double

Trella Lamson Dick

Nancy stood, her hands clasped behind her back. She watched her brother brush Dancer's golden coat. When Gary started to brush Dancer's mane, the big horse turned and nuzzled his master gently.

At last Gary set aside his brush. "There now, Dancer," he said. "You shine like the sun. And now we're going for a ride."

"Where are you going?" asked Nancy. "I want to go, too."

"I'm going through the woods and up the hill to see the eagle's nest. It's too far for you," Gary said. He put the saddle blanket on Dancer and lifted the saddle into place.

"No, it isn't," Nancy said. "Remember, I'm eight years old now. You rode Dancer when you were eight. You told me so. Dancer doesn't care if I go. Do you, Dancer?" She reached up to touch Dancer's soft mane. Dancer nickered.

"He said he would like to have me go," declared Nancy. "Please, Gary, I want to see the eagles."

"Well, go ask Mother," Gary said.

Nancy skipped across the yard to the house. In a minute she was back.

"I can go, I can go!" she said breathlessly.

"Dancer and I guessed that," laughed Gary as he cinched up the saddle. He got into the saddle and helped Nancy up behind him. They started down the lane.

The sun was hot. "Let's hurry," Nancy said. "Get up, Dancer." She kicked him in the flanks. Dancer jumped and pranced sideways.

Gary stopped Dancer and looked around at his little sister. "Don't ever do that again," he said. "I'm the pilot here. You're a passenger. There can

53

be only one pilot. Don't you forget it."

"I'm sorry," Nancy said. "I won't do it again. I promise."

Presently Gary said, "Hang on. We'll go fast."

"Oh, goody!" Nancy grabbed her brother tightly around the waist.

Gary flicked the reins. Dancer broke into a smooth gallop.

They soon came to the cool woods. Nancy kept a sharp lookout for chipmunks and squirrels. A blue jay called from a branch.

"Jay, jay, jay," Nancy called back at him.

"The woods are fun," she told Gary. "So many wonderful creatures live here."

"Shhh!" whispered Gary, stopping Dancer. "Look over that way."

Nancy peered into the shadows. Not far away stood a doe with her twin fawns. Suddenly, the doe threw up her head and dashed off through the woods. The fawns followed. They were out of sight in a minute.

"Weren't they cute with all those spots on them?" Nancy said. "I'm glad I saw them."

They passed from woods to a narrow trail leading up a hill. "See, Nancy," said Gary, "I let Dancer have his head on the hills."

"What do you mean?" asked Nancy. "Dancer has his head all the time."

Gary laughed and explained. "I leave the reins loose when we are riding up or down a hill. Then Dancer can see where he is going. He might stumble if I held his head high. Remember, on rough trails always give a horse its head."

"It sounds funny, but I'll remember," Nancy said.

They had to go slowly up the rough hill. The sun was hot. They reached the ridge at last and dismounted. The eagle's nest was in the top of a tall, dead pine tree.

"Oh, it's big!" exclaimed Nancy. "How did birds ever bring all those sticks?"

"Eagles use the same nest year after year," Gary explained. "They add a few sticks every year. That nest has been there as long as Dad can remember."

"I can't see any babies," Nancy said.

"No, it's up too high," Gary told her. "I can't

climb the tree because it isn't safe. Look, Nancy, way up in the sky. There is one of the eagles circling around. Maybe it is hunting food for the little ones."

"I do wish we could see them," Nancy said.

Gary pointed to a high rock farther up the ridge. "If I got up on it, maybe I could see if there are any little birds," he said.

They went up the ridge to the rock. Nancy waited at the base while Gary climbed it. "Can you see into the nest?" she called when he was almost to the top.

"Not yet." Gary reached for a bush to pull himself higher. A branch broke in his hand. He tumbled down the steep slope.

Nancy ran to him. "Oh, Gary, are you hurt?"

"I don't know," Gary gasped. He tried to rise. He couldn't.

"I'll help you," Nancy said, taking hold of his arm and trying to help him up.

"Don't!" Gary cried. "My knee hurts. I can't seem to straighten it."

"What shall we do?" asked Nancy, almost in

56

tears. She didn't feel so grown-up now.

Gary tried again to rise. He couldn't. "I guess we'll just stay here till somebody comes looking for us," he said.

Nancy blinked the tears out of her eyes. "Dancer and I will go get help," she said.

Gary shook his head. "You can't. You have never ridden Dancer alone."

"I can though. I know I can. The sun is so hot, and you need your knee fixed. Please, Gary, please let me go," begged Nancy.

Gary shifted his leg. The pain made him feel sick. So did the hot sun. "I guess you'll have to go," he said. "Be careful, Nancy. Don't hurry Dancer. Give him his head."

"I'll be careful. I'll remember," Nancy called as she hurried toward Dancer.

"Gary's hurt. We have to go get help," she told the horse. "You must help me."

Nancy took the reins in one hand and stood on tiptoe to reach the saddle horn with the other hand. Dancer stood very still. Nancy had to try several times before she could pull herself into the saddle.

"Come on, Dancer," she said. "Take me home as fast as you can." She pulled sharply on the reins. Dancer didn't move.

"Oh, I forgot. I have to give you your head." Nancy loosened the reins. She touched her heels to the horse's sides. Dancer began to pick his way carefully down the steep slope.

At last they were in the woods. Nancy looked around. "I don't know the way," she whispered. "Oh, Dancer, you'll have to get us out of here." She let the reins lie loose on his neck.

Dancer started off through the trees. They soon came to the highway. Nancy laughed with relief. "Now I know where we are. Good old Dancer! You are a fine pilot." She patted his neck.

A short distance down the highway, Nancy saw some men baling hay. She guided Dancer across the road and into the field.

"Hello, Nancy," one of the men said. "I didn't know you could ride Dancer alone. You're getting to be a big girl."

"Gary's hurt," Nancy answered. She began to cry.

"Hurt? How? Where is he?" asked the man.

As soon as Nancy could choke back her sobs enough to tell them, the men went into action. One went to the house to phone Nancy's mother.

"Get a blanket," called the other man. "We'll have to carry him out. I'll go see where he is." He lifted Nancy from the saddle, mounted, and helped her up behind him.

Once more Dancer, carrying double, went through the woods and up the hill. Nancy did not notice the hot sun this time. She only wanted to get to Gary. Her sudden shout of joy when she saw him made Dancer jump.

"We're back, Gary!" she called. "We got help for you."

Gary raised up on his elbow and waved.

The man got off Dancer and helped Nancy down. She ran to Gary. "They're coming to get you," she said.

Gary smiled at her. "I knew you and Dancer could make it back with help," he said.

The man looked at Gary's swollen knee. "Good thing you didn't try to walk on it," he said. "The doctor will fix it in a jiffy."

Soon the other man came with a blanket. They carried Gary gently down the hill and through the woods to a waiting truck.

"Your mother will be waiting at the doctor's," the man said. "It's lucky Nancy was along. You might have been up there for hours."

"Dancer did it," said Nancy. "He went down the hill so carefully. I didn't know the way through the woods, but Dancer did."

Gary waved good-bye and the truck sped down the highway and out of sight. Nancy once again mounted Dancer, and they followed the truck down the highway.

"Aren't you happy, Dancer?" Nancy said. "I am. I'm so happy I'd like to ride fast as the wind." Just in time she remembered she had promised Gary to be careful. She rode slowly down the highway. But when they came to the lane, she did let Dancer prance a little.

The Cow Pony

Bernadine Beatie

Rebel stood quietly in a holding pen near the auction ring. His head drooped in the August heat. He was thin. His mane and tail were matted with cockleburs. He looked old and tired. But Rebel was really only five years old.

A good judge of horses would have stopped by Rebel's pen for a second look. Rebel had powerful legs. He had a short neck. He had little fox ears. A judge of horses would have known he was a quarter horse, prized by cattlemen all over the West.

But this was dairy country. Few of the men or boys at the auction knew or cared very much about horses.

One boy did, though. He was a lad named Jodie. Jodie sat with his rancher father high up in one of the seats that surrounded the ring. Horses were a part of Jodie's life on the ranch. They were his friends, and good friends, too.

Jodie and his father had been driving home from a visit to the city when Jodie saw the auction barn.

"Let's stop, Dad," Jodie had said. "Maybe I can find a steer for my Future Farmer project."

"Not likely in dairy country," Jodie's father had said. "But we can't make it home until tomorrow, anyway. Won't hurt to stop for an hour or so."

He had pulled his pickup truck into the parking lot next to the auction barn. "Don't you go making any rash bids, Jodie," he said. "Remember how hard you worked for that fifty dollars."

"I'll remember, all right!" Jodie had grinned and followed his father into the auction barn.

Inside, bidding was slow.

"Come on, folks! Come on! Let me hear a bid,"

the auctioneer kept calling.

Each time cattle were led past Rebel's stall, he lifted an eager head. One of the handlers saw this.

"Hey, looks like there's still some life in that old nag!" he said.

The other handler laughed. "Probably just been stung by a bee."

The smell of cattle brought back happy memories to Rebel. He remembered the clean, fresh smell of the prairie after a rain. He also remembered a tall, lean man with strong, gentle hands and a sure seat in the saddle.

"Good boy, Rebel!" the man had said one day.

Rebel had pranced a bit, his head high, proud that he had cut a bawling calf from a herd of cattle.

"You'll be a real cutting horse one of these days," the man said. He brushed Rebel's buckskin coat until it shone. "We'll work again tomorrow," he promised. Then he turned Rebel into a small fenced pasture near the house.

That night, a violent spring storm swept across the prairie.

Rebel did not like being alone. His whole body quivered as lightning cut bright zigzags across the dark sky. The thunder was so loud it seemed to shake the earth.

Rebel's eyes rolled in fright. He pawed the air with his front feet.

A bolt of lightning struck nearby, and a high frightened neigh sounded in the next pasture. Rebel fled toward the sound, seeking company.

He did not sense his danger. He did not see the high barbed-wire fence before him. He crashed into it and bounced back with a scream of terror. He fell to his knees, his chest torn and bleeding.

Rebel tried to rise, but a strand of barbed wire was wrapped around his leg. During the long night, Rebel struggled to free himself. But the wire held and the barbs cut deeper and deeper.

The tall man found Rebel the next morning and cut him free. Rebel trembled with fear and pain. But the man spoke soothingly as he doctored Rebel's cuts and bandaged his leg.

Rebel's fear died away. He nuzzled at the man's shoulder and limped after him to the stable.

After that Rebel waited and waited. But the tall man with the soft voice did not return. He had sold his ranch and his livestock with it.

The new owner rounded up the horses. "We'll sell all of them that are too old to work," he said. Then he pointed at Rebel. "Sell that one, too. No place here for a horse with a bad leg!"

Then had followed Rebel's first time in the auction ring. An older man had bought him as a gift for his grandson.

"No," the boy's mother had said. "That horse limps. I know he'll trip and fall."

So Rebel was sold again—this time to a man with hard, cruel eyes. He had fastened Rebel to a cart. He had walked at Rebel's head, crying, "Nice fresh fruit for sale. Vegetables for sale."

Rebel did not have enough to eat. He grew thin. Often he closed his eyes and dreamed of the time when he lived with the tall man with the soft voice.

After that his owners were mixed up in Rebel's mind. Each time he was sold he hoped that his new owner would take him back to the land he loved. His limp was gone. He could work again. But each time Rebel had been disappointed.

Today Rebel lifted his head when he was led into the auction ring. He sniffed the air. For a split second he looked eager and alive. He looked like the horse he should have been. Then his head drooped again.

Jodie watched Rebel, and a little shiver ran up his back.

"Get that nag out of here!" someone called. And a few mocking hoots echoed from the crowd.

A boy in the front row threw an apple core at Rebel. "Let's get on with the auction!" he cried.

When the second apple core hit Rebel's flank, Jodie jumped to his feet. "Leave that horse alone!" he cried angrily.

"Want to make a bid, sonny?" the auctioneer laughed.

"Fifty dollars!" Jodie cried, standing very straight and tall.

"Sold!" the auctioneer yelled.

Jodie gulped. He had spent all his money for a horse he knew nothing about. He stole a fearful glance at his father.

"Well, Jodie," said Father, with a hint of a smile in his voice, "let's go have a look at your horse."

"Whew!" Jodie whispered softly. At least Father was not angry.

Jodie and his father were halfway down the steps when a bellow of rage sounded from below them. A huge Jersey bull was to be sold after Rebel. The bull had broken away from his handlers. He came charging into the ring, straight toward the man who was leading Rebel away.

The man gave a cry of terror and dropped Rebel's lead rope. In a flash Rebel was all cow pony. This was the work he had been born and trained to do. He whirled in his tracks. He cut right in front of the angry bull and turned him. The frightened man fled to safety.

The bull lowered his head. For a moment it looked as though he might charge through the light wooden barrier surrounding the auction ring. Then Rebel moved in, turning the bull again.

One of the bull's handlers threw open a gate. "Bring him in here, boy," he called.

Rebel understood. He whirled and turned the

bull toward the gate.

Each time the bull tried to break away, Rebel danced before him. And each time he forced the bull back toward the gate.

Finally Rebel made a quick rush. The bull swerved into the pen. The gate slammed shut.

Cheering started as the crowd jumped up. Jodie's heart hammered with excitement. It was almost like a football game. Everybody was pounding everybody else on the back and cheering Rebel.

Jodie pushed through the crowd. His father followed and stood watching as Jodie climbed into the ring and moved slowly toward Rebel.

"Hi there, boy!" Jodie said softly. He placed a gentle hand on Rebel's neck.

Rebel lifted his head and sniffed. Something about Jodie reminded him of the tall man he had known so long ago. He liked the feel of Jodie's hand. He liked the sound of his voice. He nickered softly and nuzzled Jodie. Rebel knew he was going home.

"He likes me!" Jodie said, grinning at his father.

"Yep!" Jodie's father laughed. "Son, looks like you just bought yourself a real cow pony!"

Coco, the Circus Horse

Jean Fiedler

The sound of gay music filled the circus tent. Coco, the white circus horse, tossed his head as he waited for Lady Gilda. She was the acrobat who would lead him into the ring.

But Coco's mind was not on his act with Lady Gilda. Instead, he was daydreaming his favorite dream. In this dream the star of the next act was Coco himself, and he would do his special tricks for the audience.

Mr. Jack, the trainer, blew his whistle loudly. "Now, Coco, go!" he called.

Coco stepped into the ring with Lady Gilda at his side. He cantered in time to the music. His steps were as steady and even as the ticking of a clock.

Lady Gilda jumped up onto Coco's broad back. She rode him around the ring. Then Lady Gilda twisted her body into the air and did a somersault. Coco was in just the right spot at just the right time to catch her.

Now Lady Gilda stood on Coco's back. She stood straight and tall. In an instant she had shot into the air for another somersault.

The people cheered and shouted. "Lady Gilda," they cried. "Hooray for Lady Gilda!"

Coco was glad that the people shouted and clapped for Lady Gilda. He liked Lady Gilda. She was gentle with him, and she never forgot his lump of sugar. But he did wish that just once the people would also shout, "Hooray for Coco! Hooray for the horse who does tricks!"

Coco knew how to shake hands. He could stand on his hind legs and dance to the music. He could strut and march. And he knew how to bow to an audience.

Mr. Jack had taught Coco these special tricks. Mr. Jack had said, "Someday we will make time for an extra act, and that's when we will use you, Coco."

I wish, Coco thought wistfully, *that someday would come soon!*

That night, as usual, Mr. Jack came to Coco's stall with oats and water. Coco stood up and bowed to him.

Mr. Jack laughed. "Good boy, Coco! Don't forget your tricks."

After Mr. Jack left, instead of going to sleep, Coco practiced the other tricks he had learned. There was no music, but he danced to the music in his head. There was no audience, but Coco bowed to make-believe people who shouted and clapped for him.

As the days passed, Coco dreamed more and more about performing before a real audience.

Then one day, as Lady Gilda jumped off his back, Coco forgot himself. The music sounded so gay that his feet just itched to dance. So, instead of following Lady Gilda out of the ring, as he usually did, Coco stood on his hind legs and danced in time to the music.

Coco was *so* happy to be dancing! He did not see Mr. Jack waving his arms at him from ringside. But when Mr. Jack blew his whistle, Coco scampered out of the ring. He did not take time for a bow to the audience.

Later Mr. Jack scolded Coco. He ended the scolding by saying, "Someday you will have a chance to do your tricks, but not now. You must wait, Coco. Until then, behave yourself!"

The other horses grumbled. Coco heard their grumbling.

"He was showing off, that's what he was doing," they said.

Coco was miserable. He had not meant to show off. He had simply wanted to dance. There was no way of telling that to anybody.

Now Coco began to wait for the day when he could do his tricks with Mr. Jack's permission. He waited and waited. Many days passed. But the *someday* that Mr. Jack spoke about seemed as far away as ever.

At last Coco decided sadly that he could wait no longer. The world was big. Surely *somewhere* there must be a place for him to do his own tricks and be happy.

That night, when everybody was asleep, Coco slipped out of his stall and ran away.

Far from the bright circus lights, the night was big and dark. Coco had never wandered around in the dark by himself. He ran and ran until he grew very tired. He wanted a drink of water, but there was no Mr. Jack to bring him water now.

Coco spent the night in a hayfield. The next morning he drank water from a stream and ate grass for breakfast.

Coco traveled until he came to a ranch. He saw cowboys rounding up a herd of steers. The horses had saddles of heavy leather on their backs. Coco wondered how a saddle would feel on his back.

A brown horse was standing near a fence.

"What do you do all day?" Coco asked him.

"I help the cowboys with the steers," the brown horse said. "Sometimes a steer runs off. I bring him back. What do you do?"

"I do tricks," said Coco. "I'll show you."

He danced, he bowed, he strutted, and he marched.

"Those are fine tricks," the brown horse said.

"May I stay here and do my tricks for you and the cowboys?" Coco asked hopefully.

"If you stay," said the brown horse, "you must learn to round up cattle. We are so busy we have little time for tricks here."

This was not the place for Coco. He thanked the brown horse and went on his way.

Coco came to a big stable. Many fine-looking horses were standing about.

"What do you do?" Coco asked a big gray horse.

"I am a racing horse. I run very fast, and I have won many races," the gray horse said proudly. "What do you do?"

"I do tricks," Coco said. "I'll show you."

He danced, he bowed, he strutted, and he marched.

"Those are indeed fine tricks," said the gray horse.

Once more hope filled Coco. "May I stay, then, and do tricks for you and the people here?"

But the gray horse neighed. "If you stay," he said, "you must learn to run as fast as the wind so that you can win races. Tricks don't win races."

This was not the place for Coco either. He said good-bye to the gray horse and went on his way.

Coco came to a farm. He found some grass to eat. How good one of Mr. Jack's apples would taste now. But it only made him sad to think about Mr. Jack and the circus. He was very far away from them now.

A black horse was pulling a heavy plow.

"Is this what you do all day?" Coco asked him.

"I spend my day working," said the black horse. "I help the farmer plow the field. I can pull the heaviest wagonload without getting tired." He sounded very proud. "And what do you do?"

"I do tricks," Coco said. "I'll show you."

He danced, he bowed, he strutted, and he marched.

"I have never seen such tricks," said the black horse.

And once again Coco was hopeful. "May I stay, then, and do my tricks for you and the farmer?"

"If you stay," said the black horse, "you must learn to work as I do. You must plow and pull heavy loads. There is so much work on a farm, we have no time for tricks."

"Thank you," said Coco sadly, "but I guess I'd better go on."

Tired and hungry and dirty, Coco kept going until he came to a town. There were houses and shops and people. As Coco trotted down the street, people began to follow him. Boys and girls, men and women, all followed Coco.

"I will do my tricks for the people," Coco said to himself.

He danced for them. He stood on his hind legs and pretended to shake hands. He bowed politely.

The people clapped their hands and shouted, "Hooray for the horse who does tricks!"

At last Coco's dream had come true! But something strange had happened to Coco. In spite of the clapping and the shouting, Coco was sadder than he had ever been in his life. He did not even want to do more tricks.

What's the matter with me? Coco wondered.

At this moment, a man in a blue uniform pushed through the crowd.

"Hello there, young fellow," said the man. "You look like you might be lost. But I have an idea. Follow me."

Coco followed the policeman. They went up one street and down another. Suddenly a familiar smell hit Coco's nose. He shook all over with excitement. It was the wonderful smell of animals and sawdust, peanuts and popcorn. It was the circus smell he loved!

Coco began to run as fast as he could. Sure enough, ahead of him was a big circus tent. He heard the policeman say, "This horse has been wandering around town. Does he belong to the circus?"

And then, to Coco's great joy, he saw Mr. Jack and Lady Gilda. But they did not run to him and greet him. Their faces were troubled.

At last Mr. Jack said, "I'm not sure. This horse is dirty and thin. Our Coco was a beautiful white horse."

Coco had to prove that he was Coco, and he did

it in the way he knew best. He stood on his hind legs. He shook Mr. Jack's hand. He bowed to Lady Gilda.

"Coco!" shouted Mr. Jack. "I should have known. Dirty or not, there is only one Coco." Mr. Jack hugged him as hard as he could.

Lady Gilda gave Coco two lumps of sugar.

"I missed you," she said, patting his head gently. "I always feel so safe when I somersault from your back."

Later, when Coco had been fed and watered and brushed, Mr. Jack said, "We have a surprise for you, Coco. Lady Gilda is very happy that we've found you. She likes your tricks so much that she will give up some of her time to you. You will have a special act of your own."

Joyfully Coco kicked up his heels and did a little dance. He was home again with his good friends in the circus. Coco knew this was where he belonged. He could hardly wait to begin to work on the new Coco act.

"I wonder," said Coco to himself, "if horses can learn to somersault."

A Present for Peanuts

Eva Grant

Jimmy raced his friends, Michael and David, to the Five Star Riding Stables. When he saw Mr. Barney, the owner, Jimmy skidded to a stop.

"Hi, Mr. Barney," he called out. "I'm first for Peanuts!"

Mr. Barney turned from the horse he was saddling. "Hello there, Jimmy," he said. "You sure you wouldn't want one of the other horses?"

Jimmy shook his head. "No, thanks. If I can't have Peanuts, I won't ride."

Jimmy could not forget his very first ride on a

horse. The huge white animal he had been given seemed to know he could do as he pleased. He had lowered his head and stopped to eat grass. Jimmy, panic-stricken, had found himself staring into space! It was all he could do to keep from sliding right down the horse's neck to the ground!

For a long time Jimmy had not wanted to ride.

But Peanuts had changed all that. Jimmy and Peanuts were not just rider and horse. They were friends.

When Mr. Barney led Peanuts from the stable, the horse stood quietly while Jimmy mounted. Then he rocked gently along.

Jimmy's hands on the reins felt loose and easy. When the ride was over, he hated to get off.

Michael, who was next, said, "Come on, Peanuts, let's go!"

"You'd think I had only one horse in this stable, instead of five," Mr. Barney complained. "All the kids want Peanuts."

Jimmy dismounted and Michael got on. He sat straight and tall on the horse's back.

Michael's father was a policeman and he wanted

to be one, too. Peanuts, his head high, legs dancing, stepped along like a police horse.

David was waiting when Michael returned.

"Take it easy, Davy," Mr. Barney said.

David wore cowboy boots and a cowboy hat. He leaped onto the horse's back. "Giddyap, boy," he said, touching his heels to the horse's sides. Off loped Peanuts, looking like a cow pony.

Maybe Peanuts was so popular because he seemed to know just what each child wanted him to be.

But when he came back with David, his grayish-brown coat glistened with sweat. And, trotting to his cool, dark stall, he seemed to limp a little.

There came a day when Jimmy could not have Peanuts. "He's resting," Mr. Barney said. "You'll have to take one of the other horses."

"Could I see him?" Jimmy said.

Mr. Barney nodded solemnly. He led the way to Peanuts' stall. Jimmy had never before seen Peanuts lying down.

"He's not sick, is he?" Jimmy asked.

Mr. Barney said, "I'm afraid Peanuts won't be working anymore. I've been trying to keep it a secret from you kids for as long as I could."

"What do you mean?" Jimmy said.

"His legs are growing weak. Peanuts will be fifteen years old next month," Mr. Barney replied. "Then he'll have to go. He can't do a full day's work. It wouldn't be good business for me to keep him around."

Jimmy said, "Fifteen isn't so old. My brother Bob is fifteen, and he can beat me running, hands down."

Mr. Barney smiled a little sadly. "Fifteen isn't old for a boy, but it is for a horse. Especially for a stable horse who's been used as much as Peanuts."

"Look, he's getting up!" Jimmy cried. "Here, boy, I have some sugar for you."

Peanuts stretched his head over the stall gate. His velvety muzzle found Jimmy's hand, and the sugar disappeared.

An unwelcome thought came into Jimmy's mind. He almost said, "What happens to horses when you get finished with them?" But suddenly he knew without asking.

Mr. Barney seemed to know what Jimmy was

thinking. He looked away from the stunned expression on Jimmy's face. "If someone could buy Peanuts. . . ." he began. Then he shrugged. "But who would want an old cast-off horse?"

Jimmy ran home, his heart pounding. If he was to save his friend, he would have to do something right away. Only a month until Peanuts' birthday! Once he had thought a month was a long time. Now he knew it could pass too soon.

He telephoned David and Michael. He gave them a list of names to call.

"Tell the kids we're starting a club," he said. "Meet at my house." He explained about Peanuts.

On the day of the meeting, Jimmy's living room overflowed with boys and girls of all sizes.

Jimmy took charge. They called themselves the Save Peanuts Club.

"Bring in empty cereal boxes," Jimmy told them. "You know, the round kind. And, girls, bring cloth to make banners."

The next day all the club members painted boxes and taped *Save Peanuts* signs around them.

Michael's father got permission from the police

department for the club to collect coins. Soon, on every street, boys and girls offered boxes to passers-by to be filled with pennies, nickels, and dimes.

"I'm going straight up to the houses," Jimmy said bravely. "Maybe I'll get more that way."

But when he started out, he didn't feel very brave. He saw a house with the shades pulled. *I'll try this one,* he thought, hoping a little that no one would be home.

He pushed the doorbell, and a sour-faced woman came to the door.

"What do you want?" she said, looking at his box. "You kids are always collecting for some-thing."

"It's—it's for Peanuts," Jimmy stammered.

"Peanuts! I've been asked for money for lots of things—but to buy *peanuts!* What will children think of next?" The door slammed sharply.

Jimmy stared at the closed door. He did not feel like ringing any more doorbells.

But he thought of the last time he had spoken to Mr. Barney.

"It's all arranged," the stable owner had told

him. "They'll be picking Peanuts up on the day he turns fifteen."

Jimmy made himself walk up the steps of the next house. When the door opened, he said, "We're trying to save a horse. His name is Peanuts."

Money jingled into his box.

When there was almost thirty dollars in the club treasury, Jimmy went to see Mr. Barney.

"How much would it cost to buy Peanuts?" he said.

Mr. Barney rubbed his jaw. "Well, now, that's hard to say right now," he said thoughtfully. "But, anyway, the cost is the least of it. It's the upkeep. Old horses need good food and medicine. Sometimes they need a doctor. Who's going to pay for all that?"

"I was just asking," Jimmy said, turning away with a sinking feeling.

"What are we going to do?" he asked at the next club meeting.

"I can chip in some money from my allowance," David offered.

"I don't get an allowance," Michael said. "But I

can give something from what I make on my newspaper route."

Jimmy said eagerly, "I can earn money cutting grass and pulling weeds."

The girls did not want to be left out. "We'll give part of our baby-sitting money," they promised.

Everybody talked at once.

"Then it's agreed," Jimmy said. "We're all going to go to work for Peanuts."

On the morning that Peanuts was fifteen, Jimmy awoke with a heavy feeling in his chest. He remembered it was the day the truck was coming to take the old horse away.

Jimmy dressed swiftly. Again he counted the money the children had collected. Would there be enough to save Peanuts?

Running all the way, Jimmy was the first to reach the Five Star Riding Stables. He looked around fearfully, afraid he might be too late. The pickup truck was not there yet.

Soon the others began to gather. Boys and girls came on foot and on bicycles. Some were brought in their parents' cars. By nine o'clock there was a milling crowd in front of the stable.

Mr. Barney, a puzzled look on his face, came outside.

"Where's Peanuts?" shouted the children.

The stable owner stared. Banners made from old sheets carried the words *Save Peanuts!* A table had been set up, with a huge cake in the center. On the cake were iced the words *Happy Birthday, Peanuts!*

Beside the cake were bunches of carrots, mounds of sugar cubes, and piles of apples. And leaning against the table were several bags of oats. There was more food than Peanuts could eat in a month.

"We want Peanuts!" cried the children.

Without a word Mr. Barney went inside and came out with the horse.

Jimmy stepped forward. He held out a fistful of bills. "Is this enough to buy Peanuts?" he said.

Mr. Barney said, "Looks like there's more than enough."

The children cheered.

Jimmy said, "Okay, Mr. Barney, we'll take our horse now."

Mr. Barney said, "Just a minute. Where do you

expect to keep this horse? He needs a place to live."

Jimmy swallowed hard. "Well," he said, "our club is going to work to buy his food." He looked about hopefully. "Does anyone have a place to keep Peanuts?"

Nobody answered.

Mr. Barney grinned. "You're a great bunch of kids," he said. "You didn't let Peanuts down, and I'm not going to, either. He can live here in the stable, rent free. He'll need some riding for exercise, and you can take turns doing that for him."

A shout went up from the children.

The birthday cake was cut and served. Some of the mothers had brought lemonade.

All the horses in the riding stable shared Peanuts' birthday food.

After the others had left, Jimmy and Michael and David stayed to say good-bye.

Peanuts lowered his head so the boys could hug and pet him.

It was almost as if he understood that Jimmy and his friends had given him the best present of all.

Clancy's Last Tour

Jean Lewis

Skip Semprini should have been doing his homework. Instead, he listened for the sound of hoofbeats. He listened for Clancy's hoofbeats clopping down West Forty-Fourth Street as Mounted Officer Hardy rode his beat in Times Square.

Skip closed his fourth-grade arithmetic book and picked up a shiny red apple. There would be no more apples for Clancy after today. The police horse was twenty years old and ready to retire.

Yesterday Officer Hardy had said, "I envy this horse, Skip. Up at the farm for retired police horses

Clancy will have all the hay he can eat. He'll have a warm stable in winter and acres of green pasture in summer. What a life!" He had patted Clancy's sleek side.

"Will there be somebody to give him an apple?" Skip had asked. The big, beautiful bay with the white star on his forehead ate the last bite of apple from Skip's hand.

"Up there he can pick 'em right off the trees. They've got an apple orchard the size of Central Park," Officer Hardy had answered.

Clop, clop, cloppety, clop.

Skip jumped up. He grabbed his wooden shoe-shine box. The door slammed behind him, and he clattered down the three flights of stairs to the street door. It was four-thirty and his mother would not be home from work for another hour.

Taking the broad brownstone steps two at a time, Skip waved to Officer Hardy. The policeman saluted in return.

For the past two years every afternoon at four-thirty, Skip had met Officer Hardy and Clancy in front of his house. Then he walked beside them two blocks east to the Times Square theater district, where the officer began his eight-hour tour of duty.

This afternoon both man and boy were silent. Clancy nudged Skip's pocket, begging for his apple. He knew he would not get it till later, but he always asked anyway.

Theaters lined both sides of West Forty-Fourth Street. Today was Wednesday and the afternoon performances were just letting out.

Crowds milled about the sidewalks, spilling into the street. Taxis and cars crawled east on Forty-Fourth Street, two abreast.

Officer Hardy, on Clancy, rode up and down, gently but firmly keeping the crowds from blocking traffic.

As usual, Skip placed his shoeshine box beside the gray walls of the Paramount Theater Building.

Did Clancy know this was his last working day? Skip wondered. If he did, he did not show it. His coat shone like a colt's. And his neck arched gracefully to the gentle pressure of Officer Hardy's reins.

"Okay, kid. Shine 'em up!"

Skip had a customer. He turned from watching

Clancy to go to work on the man's brown loafers.

It was not the smell of the polish that blurred his eyes and tightened his throat. It was the thought that tomorrow he would be here and Officer Hardy would be here but that Clancy would not. Officer Hardy would be on a new mount, a horse that would take Clancy's place.

"Holdup!" yelled someone across the street.

"I've got to see this! Keep the change!" said Skip's customer. He flung a dollar bill at Skip and raced for Shubert Alley.

Skip could see Officer Hardy on Clancy galloping through the alley connecting Forty-Fourth and Forty-Fifth Streets. He was blowing his whistle shrilly. Skip followed, on the run.

On Forty-Fifth Street he saw Mr. Miller, manager of the three-floor car-park next to the hotel.

Mr. Miller waved excitedly. "There he goes! Through the lobby! Stop him!"

Officer Hardy dismounted, looping Clancy's reins over a hook just inside the entrance to the car-park. Still blowing his whistle, he drew his gun and dived through the hotel's revolving door.

The attendants at the car-park, where the robbery had taken place, joined the crowd around the hotel.

Skip glanced back toward Clancy just in time to see him rising slowly in midair! He had stepped onto one of the huge car elevators, but he was still hitched to the hook. Somehow the elevator had started up!

If Clancy was not freed right away, his head might be crushed by the rising elevator!

Skip threw himself into untying Clancy's reins. Then he jumped up on the elevator beside the horse, pulling him back in.

The big bay gratefully nuzzled the boy's shoulder while Skip stroked his neck. Skip was shaking. He leaned against Clancy's warm body.

The elevator stopped at the top floor and Skip led Clancy off. He knew he should take him right back down, but he wanted to be alone with his friend for just a little while. He wanted to say good-bye alone.

He fed Clancy his apple. Then, standing on a car fender, he climbed into the saddle. The stirrups were too long. He climbed down to shorten them and got up again on Clancy's broad back.

Several times Officer Hardy had taken Skip to visit his brother's riding stable on Staten Island. There Skip had learned how to hold the reins and to sit properly in the saddle. But this was his very first time up on Clancy.

Even Clancy seemed surprised. He looked around at his rider as if to say, "Well, what are *you* doing up there?"

Suddenly Skip buried his face in the horse's velvety neck. "Oh, Clancy, please don't go," he whispered. Clancy whinnied comfortingly.

Skip did not know how long he sat there in the dark, his hot face pressed against Clancy's neck. Suddenly a light flashed in his eyes.

"Skip!" said Officer Hardy. "I've been looking all over for Clancy. After I made the arrest and the patrol car picked up the thief, I came back for Clancy. When I couldn't find him I was afraid he'd run off and got himself hurt!"

Officer Hardy sounded both relieved and angry. Relieved to find Clancy, angry to find Skip with him this way.

"Did you lead him up here?" Officer Hardy asked.

Skip nodded. He could not find his voice to answer.

"Why?" asked the policeman.

Skip scrambled down and walked to the elevator without replying.

At the street level, Sam, one of the attendants, stopped them. "Well, Officer, when does this kid get his medal?"

"What medal? For horse stealing?" snapped the policeman. Skip winced.

"For horse *saving*," corrected Sam. Then he described what he had seen earlier, how Skip's swift action had saved Clancy from serious injury.

Officer Hardy turned to the boy. "Skip, thanks. Just forget what I said. Okay? I'm very grateful."

"I should have brought him back right away," said Skip. "I just wanted to tell him good-bye." Then he felt the policeman's arm around his shoulder, patting it, hard.

"Better get home now," Officer Hardy said gruffly. "I'm off Saturday. Meet me at the ten o'clock ferry and we'll go over to my brother's place. Okay?"

Skip nodded and started walking west very quickly. He did not want to turn for his last look at Clancy. At Eighth Avenue he broke into a run, never stopping till he threw himself onto his own bed. He buried his face in his pillow.

On Saturday Joe Hardy greeted them out at the stables. "We've got a couple of new ones since last time, Skip."

In the first stall was a frisky little black filly. She tossed her mane briskly at Skip.

"And over here. . . ."

Skip froze. In the second stall stood a horse who was the living image of . . . yes, it was! Clancy!

"*Clancy!* They let you keep him?" gasped Skip.

"When I told the lieutenant how you rescued him, he said he couldn't send Clancy to the farm," said Officer Hardy.

The policeman's brother laughed. "He's trying to tell you Clancy is yours, Skip. All yours. You can come over and ride him any time you like. And don't worry about the feed bill. It's on the house, for keeps!"

Skip did not dare move. If he did, he might wake up! This must surely be a dream!

"Well, you know how to get on a horse," said Officer Hardy gruffly. "Let's see you do it."

Skip moved and found he was not dreaming after all. He was wide awake!

From then on, instead of Skip waiting for Clancy, Clancy waited for Skip out at Hardy's Riding Academy. Every Saturday and Sunday during the school year and every day in the summer they were together. Clancy was Skip's horse now . . . for keeps.

Little Con

Ellen Dolan

Danny had been staying at his Uncle Mike's farm in County Galway, Ireland, for two days when the gypsy wagons came by. Already Danny was missing his friends from the city. He was glad for a little excitement.

"Uncle Mike, come look at the gypsies," cried Danny.

"I'm busy," said Uncle Mike. But he came over anyway.

At first all Danny saw were the bright wagons and the gypsy children. But then his eyes widened. Tied to the back of one of the wagons was a small gray pony. His coat was very dusty, but he held his head proudly.

"What a beautiful pony!" said Danny.

"Beautiful!" said his uncle scornfully. "It's only a gypsy nag."

"I wish you had a pony on the farm," said Danny wistfully.

"Do you, now?" answered Uncle Mike. "Well, I don't like the looks of the stick the man carries. And I don't like the bruises on the pony's back. It might be better if he did live on the farm."

"Oh, Uncle Mike," said Danny, laughing. "You didn't like the looks of my skinny legs, and here I am fattening up at your farm. If you're not careful, you'll have all of Ireland with you."

"Well, do you want the pony or not?" asked Uncle Mike, pretending to be angry.

"Oh, yes, please," said Danny.

Uncle Mike went to talk to the gypsies. Danny waited impatiently. But soon his uncle gave one of the men some money, and the man untied the small pony.

When his uncle led the pony into the farmyard and dropped the rope, the pony walked right up to Danny.

"He comes from the Connemara hills," said the gypsy shortly, "and I wish you luck with the lazy brute." He turned to Uncle Mike. "Don't forget our bargain. We can camp behind your barley field for a few weeks."

"Mind you stamp out your fires," said Uncle Mike.

But the gypsy just waved a hand and drove off.

Danny hardly saw the gypsies leave. A real pony! And it was *his!*

"When I get you brushed, you're going to be the finest-looking pony in the county," said Danny. "But you must have a name. Since you came from Connemara, I'll call you 'Little Con.' What fun we are going to have."

He would not miss his city friends so much now, he knew.

Little Con was feeling happy, too. Here was somebody near his size. And he did not carry a big black stick. As soon as Danny began to care for his bruises, Little Con knew he had a good master.

"Everyone who lives on the farm must work," Danny said one day when Little Con's bruises were healed.

Little Con seemed to understand. He wanted to be useful.

"Uncle Mike says we can gather peat for fuel," Danny said.

So from then on twice a week Danny hitched Little Con to a cart and they went to the peat bog.

There was only one bad place on the way. At the bottom of the hill near the farm was an old wooden bridge. Little Con had caught his left fore-leg between two planks when he had crossed it with the gypsies. He never came to that bridge again without being afraid. He always stopped.

Danny did not know *why* Little Con stopped. But each time he patiently climbed down from the cart. He patted the pony's neck and talked gently to him.

"Easy, lad. Good lad. Come along now. I'll lead you across." And before Little Con knew it, he was across the bridge.

The rest of the trip was always fun. Soon they passed the neighboring farm. It belonged to Mr.

Clifton, who trained horses for Ireland's famous steeplechase races.

"You must look trim now for Mr. Clifton. He knows a good pony when he sees one," said Danny.

The pride in Danny's voice always made Little Con raise his head and step smartly.

If they were lucky Little Con would catch a glimpse of the horses and ponies staying at Mr. Clifton's farm. Danny might see Mr. Clifton's sons, who were about his own age, sliding down the haystacks. He longed to wave to them, but—would they care for a city boy? Danny wasn't sure.

Then Little Con and Danny hurried on to the bog. While Danny cut the peat and loaded it in the cart, Little Con waited quietly beside the road.

Sometimes he nibbled grass. Other times he looked up at the hills, where he had lived before the gypsies caught him. Then his legs would tremble and he would wish he were racing with the other wild ponies again. He remembered leaping over stones and streams with the wind in his face. The only pasture Uncle Mike could spare for Little Con was too small for a good run, so he did not get much exercise anymore. He was always glad to get out for the trip to the bog. Except for that bridge!

Every evening after dinner Danny came to sit by Little Con. They both liked this part of the day.

One very hot night Danny could not eat much and came out earlier than usual. Little Con seemed hot, too. He stamped his hooves and tossed his head. Danny watched him a bit and then turned the way Little Con was looking.

Down beyond the barley field there was a blur of color and movement. The gypsies were leaving their camp. Danny sat down with relief. He had been a little worried that the gypsies might want Little Con back if they saw how much better he looked now.

"Don't worry, Little Con. They can't hurt you anymore," he said.

But Little Con still stamped his hooves. Something besides the heat or the gypsies was bothering him. Danny looked again to be sure the gypsies were gone.

Suddenly he leaped to his feet. The last gypsy wagon was just going over the hill. Behind it at the edge of the field puffs of smoke were rising.

"Uncle Mike," yelled Danny. "The barley field is on fire!"

Uncle Mike ran out of the house, took one look, and shook his fist. "Oh, those gypsy rascals! I told them to put out their fires!"

He ran to the barn for some sacks. While he was soaking them in water he called to Danny.

"We must have help. Mr. Clifton has plenty of men. If you hurry, we might stop the fire before it gets to the roof of the house."

Danny jumped on Little Con and they galloped out the gate. Little Con was glad to get away from that fire and he ran at full speed. Down the hill they went, lickety-split.

Straight ahead was the wooden bridge.

Little Con knew Danny was in a hurry. There was no time now for him to get down and lead him across the bridge. For one moment Little Con paused. Then he turned off the road and ran down to the edge of the stream that ran under the bridge.

"Stop, Little Con! Where are you going?" cried Danny.

Little Con tossed his head as if to say, "Hold on. I know what I am doing."

The pony gave one powerful push with his legs, and then he was flying over the stream. Th-rump! Horse and rider landed safely on the grassy bank on the other side!

Danny slid about a bit on his pony's back, but he had a good grip on the mane. "Little Con," he gasped, "I didn't know you could jump. Oh, you are a wonderful pony!"

Little Con did not even slow down. Up the bank he went, over a small hedge, and back to the road.

When Danny realized Little Con could *jump* over anything in the way, he said, "It will be shorter to cut through the fields. This way, Little Con. Hurry! Fast as you can go!"

Once Little Con was sure Danny could stay on his back he did not stop for anything. Away they went over stone walls and small streams, over rocks and hedges. With his head up and his legs stretched out, Little Con was running as he had in the hills. Soon they were pounding into Mr. Clifton's yard.

Mr. Clifton ran to meet them. "What is it, boy?"

Quickly Danny told him about the fire. Mr. Clifton shouted to his sons and the men. In a few minutes they were on their horses and ready to go.

"Lead the way with your pony, lad," said Mr. Clifton.

Danny was afraid Little Con would be tired. He need not have worried. Little Con started back across the fields as fast as he had come. He guided the other horses around the larger rocks and away from low branches. But still he did not slow down. Little Con was having fun!

Almost too soon for Little Con they were back at the farm. Uncle Mike looked up in surprise.

"That was quick work. Good lad, Danny. Good lad, Little Con."

While Danny and Mr. Clifton's boys took charge of the horses, the men ran to help Uncle Mike. With so many working, they had the fire out very quickly. And because Danny and Little Con had been so fast, they saved not only the house but most of the barley as well.

At last Uncle Mike and Mr. Clifton came over to Danny and Little Con.

"I've seen many races in my life," Mr. Clifton said, "but never a finer one than today. This is a remarkable pony."

"Little Con? Our gypsy nag?" said Uncle Mike.

"Gypsy nag!" said Mr. Clifton. "With a little work he could be a champion."

The words sang inside Danny. "A champion! I knew it!"

But Mr. Clifton was still talking. "Danny, could you bring Little Con over every morning and let me train him? My boys would be glad for your company and you would be back in the afternoon to help your uncle. And I promise you that the first race your pony wins will more than pay for the barley lost in the fire."

With his arm tight around Little Con's neck, Danny just stared at Mr. Clifton. He looked at the shy, friendly faces of the two boys, then at his uncle, then back at the boys. The boys grinned.

Uncle Mike smiled. "Would you like that, Danny?"

Danny smiled back. His face was full of excitement. "We'd love it," he said.

Partners

Jean Lewis

Tim glanced at the silk-hatted driver beside him, remembering that even Rosy had looked astonished when they arrived together at Nix's Stable that morning. Tim cringed as he recalled introducing his sister to the other drivers.

"This is my sister, Irene. Mac's sick, and she's going to drive Rosy till he gets well."

The older men shook their heads, and the younger ones whistled.

Mr. Nix, the stable owner, looked doubtful. "Old horses and new drivers don't mix," he grumbled.

"Remember what happened with Maria?"

Tim had thought of nothing else ever since the doctor told them their grandfather's heart attack could mean that he might never again drive for a living.

Mr. Linguitti, another driver at the stable, and Maria had worked together for years. When Mr. Linguitti retired, Maria wouldn't work with any of the other men. She did all kinds of crazy things, until finally Mr. Nix had to "get rid of her." Mac never explained just what that meant, but Tim was sure Irene's tale of Maria at a lovely farm for old horses was just made up to keep him from finding out the sad truth. And now the same thing could happen to Rosy!

The look on Tim's face as he remembered Maria's fate caused Mr. Nix's usually gruff voice to soften a bit. "I'll try you out for a couple of days, Irene," he said. "You've ridden the rig a lot, alongside your grandfather, but *he's* the one should be drivin'." He pointed to Tim. "Never missed a Saturday out with Mac, that one."

Tim tried not to show how proud Mr. Nix's words

made him. But the fact remained that ten-year-olds weren't allowed to drive. Big sisters had all the luck.

Grandfather Macauley had been both father and mother to Tim and Irene ever since their parents died in a car crash. Before Tim was old enough to go to the stable, Irene accompanied their grandfather. When she reached eighteen, she seemed to outgrow horses—something Tim knew could never happen to him.

After that, every Saturday morning and all during school vacations, Tim would walk with Grandfather Macauley to Nix's Stable. He would help hitch Rosy, the dapple-gray mare, to the open carriage with the shiny red leather cushions. After he'd filled Rosy's feed bag with oats for lunch, he'd climb up beside his grandfather on the driver's seat. With a gentle slap of the reins on Rosy's broad back, they'd ride off across town to work.

Tim's grandfather was "Mac" to the other drivers parked along Fifty-Ninth Street near Fifth Avenue. They were all in the same business—taking out-of-town visitors for carriage rides through New York's

Central Park—but to Mac his job was a special partnership, one in which Rosy shared equally.

"Imagine!" he would say, nodding toward the other men. "They don't even bother to take out the same horse every day. They're not on *speakin'* terms!"

Tim knew how proud his grandfather was that he and Rosy were "a team."

"It's the only way," Mac would say, tilting his battered silk hat, and Rosy would toss her head in agreement.

For over thirty years, twelve of them with Rosy, Mac had been driving his customers through Central Park. This was the first April starting date he'd ever missed.

Tim and Irene arrived too late for the best parking spaces. These were in front of the Plaza Hotel, where very rich out-of-towners and many movie stars stayed. The wheels screeched against the curb as Irene edged the carriage into the only space left. It was a tight squeeze, especially for Rosy. She could barely stretch her neck without bumping the back of the carriage in front of her.

Irene reached for the guitar on the seat beside her. "You'll see," she had told Tim that morning as they left the house. "My folk songs will attract lots of customers."

As Irene tuned her guitar, Rosy's ears twitched. Then Irene began to sing mournfully about "the foggy, foggy dew," and Rosy looked back, her eyes rolling wildly. Tim shifted uneasily. Couldn't Irene see that Rosy was not a folk song fan?

Rosy whinnied, but Irene sang on, and a young couple stopped to listen. Irene smiled smugly at Tim, but after his years on the driver's seat with Mac, Tim could spot "lookers" as quickly as his grandfather. This stringy-haired pair was not going to pay five dollars for a carriage ride, no matter how much they "dug" Irene's singing.

Suddenly Irene hit a quavering high note. Just as suddenly, Rosy hit an even higher one, then plunged the wrong way into the one-way traffic barreling down Fifth Avenue!

As Irene grabbed for the reins, her guitar flew out of her hands and onto the hood of a passing

Volkswagen. Although Tim had caught hold of the reins, his eighty pounds were no match for runaway Rosy. Together, they finally brought Rosy to a halt, just as Mounted Officer Carney reined up beside them.

"If I didn't know your grandfather so well, young lady," said the policeman sternly, "I'd write you out a ticket. Just remember that guitar playing and carriage driving don't mix. I'll have my eye on you."

Luckily, Irene's smashed guitar was the only serious casualty. Neither Rosy nor the carriage was even scratched, and Tim and Irene were only shaken up.

As they rode in silence back down to Fifty-Ninth Street, Tim was wondering what Mr. Nix would have to say. And how were they going to tell their grandfather?

"Irene, I'm countin' on you and Tim to hold the fort till I get back on my feet again," Mac had told them that morning. "I don't want one of them lunkhead drivers yankin' Rosy's mouth sore. I know you'll take good care of her."

Now Mr. Nix might never trust them with the

rig again. And what would happen to Rosy? Tim shivered as Irene pulled up in a patch of bright spring sunshine near the park entrance. Some of the younger horses in the lineup pranced a bit and tossed their manes.

Whole families were out enjoying the spring vacation. As Tim stood stroking Rosy's nose and feeding her lump sugar, a family of out-of-towners stopped by. No one could imagine Rosy as a runaway now.

"Can I pat her?" asked the smallest tourist.

"Sure," said Tim, gently pulling the mare's head down to within reach of the delighted little girl.

They were the first customers of the day.

As they clip-clopped through the park, Irene pointed out the sights with a long-handled buggy whip—the bright curlicue roofs of the Children's Zoo, Hans Christian Andersen's fairy-tale characters grouped in bronze on the grass, the gaily fluttering banners of the Theater-in-the-Park.

At Seventy-Second Street they slowed at the sight of some unusual activity. Tim saw people standing under the trees, near a couple of parked station wagons and a truck filled with equipment.

"And over there, they're filming a movie," commented Irene, just as though this happened every day.

"Can we watch?" begged the little girl.

Irene pulled over to the side of the road, where they had a grandstand view.

"It's Colonel Korn from 'Caraway Square'—on TV!" exclaimed the little girl excitedly.

Tim recognized the star of TV's most popular program for youngsters. Dressed in his familiar broad-brimmed hat and bush jacket, Colonel Korn sat on a rock, feeding nuts to a band of chittering squirrels.

"Hi, Colonel Korn!" called the little girl, leaning over the side of the carriage. "I watch you on TV every Saturday morning in Indianapolis!"

The cameraman turned around to grin, and the colonel waved. Then he strolled over to the carriage.

"What a pretty horse," he said, offering Rosy an apple. He stroked her nose. "What's her name?"

When Tim told him, he said, "Maybe we could work her into one of our shows sometime."

The cameraman called out that he was ready for the next sequence, and the colonel said good-bye.

As Irene drove the sightseers back to Fifty-Ninth Street, the little girl sighed, "Just think! I met Colonel Korn in Central Park—*live!*"

Back at the stable, Mr. Nix said just what Tim feared he would say. "Sorry, but I can't trust you kids with the rig. If Mac isn't well enough to drive Rosy by next week—" He shrugged. "Old horses and new drivers just plain don't mix."

Tim emptied his pockets of all the sugar he had left and gave it to Rosy. He stayed with her long after she'd eaten it, until finally Irene hustled him off to supper.

"Couldn't we buy her?" Tim pleaded on the way home.

Irene shook her head. "You know Mac couldn't afford that, especially now, with all the doctor bills to be paid."

"If Mr. Nix is going to—" Tim swallowed hard— "to get rid of her anyway, wouldn't he just as soon give her to us?"

"Where would we keep a horse? In our apartment? We'd have to pay Mr. Nix to stable her, and we just haven't got the money, Tim," said Irene, sounding dismally grown-up.

Then they agreed that Mac mustn't know they had been fired. Not yet. So, the next three mornings, they left the house on schedule, just as though they were going to the stable. Instead, they rode the ferry to Staten Island and took long walks through the countryside that lay just twenty minutes away from lower Manhattan. And at supper they invented stories to tell Mac about the customers they'd driven each day.

On the fourth day, Tim and Irene went to Central Park. There was a folk song festival that Irene wanted to attend, and Tim brought his roller skates. Some boys from school were playing hockey at Wollman Rink, and he'd promised to come. What he really wanted to do was to go over to the stable and see Rosy, but Irene wouldn't let him.

"It won't do you or Rosy any good, Tim," she advised. "Try to forget about her."

No matter where he was, Tim knew he could never

do that. He'd never forget Rosy.

As they entered the park at Fifty-Ninth Street, one of the drivers stopped them to ask about Mac.

"He's much better," Irene answered, "but the doctor says he can't ever work full time again."

"That's a shame," he said. Then he added, "Say, there's a man been looking for you two." The driver pointed. "That's him."

It was Colonel Korn, just coming down the steps of the Plaza Hotel. He caught sight of them, waved, and hurried over.

"Just the two people I want to see!" he exclaimed. "But Rosy's the one I really want to talk to. I'd like her to costar with me on 'Caraway Square' this summer. Where is she?"

"I guess she's still at the stable," said Tim. Then he found himself telling the colonel all about Mac's being sick, Rosy's running away, and Mr. Nix's planning to get rid of Rosy.

Before he'd finished, the colonel was bundling them into a taxi.

"Give him the address of the stable," Korn told Irene. Then he explained why he'd been looking for them. "After I saw you in the park the other day, we decided to use a horse and carriage like yours in next season's series. Each week we'll stop at a different place in the park—the mounted police stables, the outdoor theater, the Children's Zoo. We'll bring this beautiful park to children all over the country, and we'll film all the shows right here this summer. I had only one doubt about Rosy. How such a gentle horse could play a runaway. That's what she does in the opening show. I jump up and stop her, and that's how we get acquainted. But now I know that all we have to do is to let Irene sing about the 'foggy, foggy dew,' and off goes Rosy!"

Tim was too worried to respond to the colonel's effort to cheer him up. Would they be in time to save Rosy?

When they arrived at the stable, they found Rosy's stall empty. Tim raced upstairs to Mr. Nix's office, followed by Irene and Colonel Korn.

"Rosy!" he gasped.

"Where's Rosy?" they all chorused.

Mr. Nix shook his head and led Tim to the window. He pointed to a horse and carriage heading up the street. The horse was Rosy, and the driver was Mac.

"Mac came over to surprise you today. His first day out," said Mr. Nix. "When he heard what had happened, he insisted on goin' right back to work— to save Rosy. I never saw so many people worried about one horse!"

All that summer, Mac and Rosy worked together with Colonel Korn in the park, filming "Caraway Square." The TV people had bought Rosy and the carriage from Mr. Nix and hired Mac to drive. He didn't have to work all day—not even every day.

"Just enough to be good for him," everyone agreed.

As he drove Rosy through the park he knew so well, Mac still told the viewers about all the special places. "Tim," he chuckled, "I'm paid ten times as much now for doin' just what I've been doin' for thirty years!"

It was a wonderful summer, and when it was over, Colonel Korn gave Rosy and the carriage to Mac.

"Thank you," beamed Mac. "With the salary

you've paid me, Rosy can stay on at Nix's Stable forever as a payin' guest—except now that she's a TV star, she might want to move right into the Plaza Hotel!"

When school started, every Saturday, just as before, Tim and Mac would pick up Rosy and drive to the park.

They never lacked for customers. "There's Mac and Rosy from TV!" the youngsters would exclaim.

"Partners," the old man would say, giving the reins a gentle slap. "It's the only way!"

And Rosy would toss her head in agreement.

Golden Ghost Stallion

Sharon Wagner

"Do you think he'll come to the knoll this evening like he did yesterday?" Beth asked Chuck as they sat together on the back porch of their small cabin.

Chuck, who was ten, seemed to consider the question for a minute, then shook his head. "Corey says no. The stallion only shows up around here every two or three years. Somebody gets a glimpse of him, and then he disappears again. That's why they call him the Golden Ghost."

"He sure is pretty." At nine, Beth was more interested in watching for the beautiful palomino stallion than in exploring the corrals, pools, streams, and forests that her brother found so fascinating. They'd been at the Glacier Mountain Dude Ranch for three days now, and already Beth was dreading the end of their two-week vacation, when their parents would take them back to town. That meant that horses and riding would once more be reserved for weekends.

"There are lots of stories about him," Chuck went on. "The ranch hands were telling me about the roundups of wild horses. Corey says he saw the herd once, but no one's ever gotten close enough to take a single mare away from the Golden Ghost."

"I wish he would come back," Beth said, her eyes on the knoll behind the corrals, where just last evening she'd seen the big stallion outlined against the dark green of the Montana forest.

"Corey says he'd better not come sniffing around anymore," Chuck murmured.

"Why not?"

"He's liable to get shot." Chuck was standing at the porch rail now, squinting against the rays of the setting sun.

130

"Who'd shoot him?" Beth was shocked at the idea.

"The owner of the ranch. He's ordered Corey and the other cowboys to kill the stallion if he keeps coming back."

"But why?" Beth's too-vivid imagination pictured the proud stallion shot and falling.

"Mr. Buckley has some real valuable horses, and he's afraid that the stallion wants to steal them. I guess it's happened before."

"Why don't they just try to catch him?" Beth asked. "He's so beautiful that he must be valuable, too."

Chuck's only answer was a shrug; then suddenly he stiffened. "Look," he whispered, pointing to the knoll.

The brush stirred a little, then parted, and the big horse stepped out into plain view. His golden coat caught the sun's rays, and his long, silvery mane moved in the evening breeze. Beth gasped with pleasure and awe. His ringing, challenging neigh echoed across the entire ranch. Almost at once there were answering whinnies and squeals from the corral. Then a shot rang out, and the stallion disappeared into the brush once more.

"Did they hit him?" Beth asked, hoping that Chuck could tell her.

"I'll bet they only shot into the air," Chuck said. "None of the cowboys wants to shoot him."

"I don't suppose he'll ever come back now," Beth said sadly. Their mother called them then, to come inside and change for dinner.

The evening passed quickly, what with the campfire songs and the tall tales the cowboys loved to tell. The next day was busy, too, but as evening came, Beth and Chuck found themselves once more on the porch, watching the knoll. "You don't think he'll come, do you?" Beth asked anxiously.

"Everybody says he won't," Chuck said, "but I think he will."

"We can't let him get shot," Beth said. "I heard Mr. Buckley promise a reward to the man who gets rid of him."

"So what can we do?" Chuck asked.

Beth hesitated. Her brother was inclined to laugh at her suggestions, but this was too important for her to worry about his teasing. "I think we should go up on the knoll and wait for him," she said.

"What?" Chuck was too surprised to laugh.

"I think he's coming here for a reason, and I don't mean stealing the mares, either. I think he wants someone to come after him."

Chuck shook his head, and his glance told her that he thought she was weird—but he got to his feet. "We can hike to the knoll," he said. "If we're there, he probably won't come, and then, at least, no one will take a shot at him."

It was cool under the tall pines that fringed the knoll, and Beth enjoyed sitting there after their short hike. She'd almost forgotten their reason for coming, when the soft rhythm of hooves trotting over pine needles brought Chuck to his knees. Because they were well shielded by brush and wild rosebushes, the stallion was almost even with them when they stood up.

The Golden Ghost stopped short and snorted, his ears flicking back and forth questioningly, his large dark eyes studying them without fear. At close range, the marks of his wild living were obvious in his

ungroomed coat and wind-tangled mane and tail.
He was still beautiful, and Beth felt a thrill of excitement rather than fright. She stepped across the narrow space between the rosebushes and the large pine
she and Chuck had been under.

"You mustn't go out there, Ghost," she said.
"They'll shoot you if you do. Take your herd and go
back into the mountains, where it's safe."

The horse stood there, his dark eyes somehow
pleading; then he turned and started back the way
he'd come. He took three steps, then looked back. A
whicker, low and friendly, seemed to reach out to
Beth and Chuck.

"He wants us to come with him," Beth said.

"I don't know . . ." Chuck said. "Corey and the
other cowboys say he's a killler; that's why nobody
tries to capture him anymore."

"Does he look mean to you?" Beth asked, not
bothering to wait for an answer. Usually she re-
spected Chuck's opinions, but this time she knew
she was right. As if to prove her point, the stallion
set off at a walk, leading the way.

It was nearly dark by the time the stallion stopped

leading them and whinnied. An answer came, seemingly from right at their feet. Beth looked down, and, in the last glow of twilight, she saw two shapes in a deep ravine that opened not ten feet ahead. The bigger of the shapes was a mare, and beside her stood a tiny foal.

"What's the matter, girl?" Beth called, moving cautiously to the edge of the ravine.

"She's trapped down there with her foal," Chuck said. "See; they must have fallen in over on that side, where the ground is all torn up."

Beth nodded, at the same time realizing that what she'd thought was a ravine was really a deep pocket in the mountain earth. Three sides of it rose as steeply as cliffs. The entrance had been blocked by a landslide. "What'll we do?" she asked.

"I'll go back to the ranch and get Corey," Chuck answered. "Maybe he can get them out. Do you think you could wait here? I'm not sure I can find my way back without something to guide me."

"How will I guide you?" Beth asked skeptically. She didn't like the idea of being left in the dark forest all alone.

"I'll build a little fire right up on the rocks," Chuck said. "But you'll have to stay and watch it. You know how dangerous it is to have a fire among the trees."

Despite the fire, Beth was apprehensive as she watched her brother leave. She turned her attention to the horses below, trying to think of them instead of the night around her. The fire's glow showed the fall of timber and rock blocking the fourth side of the ravine; but more than that, it showed the thin, hungry look of the mare and the smallness of her foal.

A soft sound behind her brought Beth around nervously, but it was only the golden stallion. "She's one of your mares, isn't she?" Beth asked, taking a step toward the horse. "That's why you came back, even after they shot at you. You were calling for someone to come and help her, weren't you?"

The fact that the stallion stayed nearby for almost an hour, until there was a distant sound of hoofbeats, told Beth she was right. He whinnied once more, then whirled and disappeared at a gallop into the forest. Sadly Beth watched him go, but she had little time to wonder about him. In a few moments, three riders—Chuck, Corey, and another cowboy—arrived and dismounted.

Corey looked the situation over quickly, using a big flashlight to examine first the mare and foal, then the barrier of broken trees and stone at the far end of the ravine. "She's weak," he said. "Been without food and water for a few days, but I think she's got a good chance if we can get her out tonight."

"What about the foal?" Chuck asked.

"It'll need lots of care, but it should make it, too." Corey leaned so far over the lip of the ravine that Beth was afraid he'd fall. Then he stood up, grinning. "That's Tango, my mare. I thought she was dead."

As he and the other cowboy, with Chuck helping, began work on the heavy tree trunks, roping them and letting their horses drag them away, Corey shouted the story to Beth. He'd turned Tango out with the dude horses—two years ago—and that spring, she'd been missing. He'd searched the range without finding her and had finally given up.

It was very late by the time a narrow space had been cleared and Corey could ride down into the ravine. For a moment Beth was afraid that the mare might fight and make her rescue impossible, but she seemed to remember Corey, and in a little while he was leading her and the foal, slowly and carefully, through the opening and down the long trail to the ranch. Beth, riding double with Chuck, followed happily.

Beth and Chuck didn't go on the picnic ride the next day with the other guests; instead they stayed in the small corral with Corey, helping him care for Tango and the foal. Both had cuts and scratches from their fall down into the ravine. Laying his hand gently on the mare's head, Corey said, "They'll need lots of petting, too, to get used to being with people."

It was just about sunset when Beth suddenly looked toward the knoll. "Look!" she said. The Golden Ghost stood there, not calling this time— only watching them. "He came to make sure they're all right," Beth said.

Corey nodded. "Guess we won't be seeing him again for a year or two," he said. "Now he knows they're safe."

"I'll never forget him," Beth said, watching

somberly as the golden horse lost himself in the shadows.

"I guess not," Corey said. "I talked to your parents this afternoon, and they gave me permission to do something."

"What's that?" Chuck asked.

"Well, if it hadn't been for you two, I'd never have found Tango. She and her foal would have died in another day or two, so I think you should have a reward."

Beth looked up from stroking the foal's fuzzy neck. "A reward?"

Corey nodded. "How would you like to have this little filly? It'll be six months before she can leave her mother, but your father said he'd rent a trailer and come back for her then—if you two want her."

"*Want* her!" Beth didn't have to look at Chuck to know what his answer would be. Anyway, she was busy hugging the filly and trying to hold back her happy tears. Owning Tango's little Ghost was all of her dreams come true.

YOU WILL ENJOY

THE TRIXIE BELDEN SERIES

28 Exciting Titles

THE MEG MYSTERIES

6 Baffling Adventures

ALSO AVAILABLE

Algonquin
Alice in Wonderland
A Batch of the Best
More of the Best
Still More of the Best
Black Beauty
The Call of the Wild
Dr. Jekyll and Mr. Hyde
Frankenstein
Golden Prize
Gypsy from Nowhere
Gypsy and Nimblefoot
Lassie—Lost in the Snow
Lassie—The Mystery of Bristlecone Pine
Lassie—The Secret of the Smelters' Cave
Lassie—Trouble at Panter's Lake
Match Point
Seven Great Detective Stories
Sherlock Holmes
Shudders
Tales of Time and Space
Tee-Bo and the Persnickety Prowler
Tee-Bo in the Great Hort Hunt
That's Our Cleo
The War of the Worlds
The Wonderful Wizard of Oz